Knowledge

Knowledge

(Advice for Life)

John E. Neirinckx II

***

Copyright © 2021 by John E. Neirinckx II

All rights reserved, including the right to reproduce this book or portions thereof in any form whatsoever.

To order books or other products contact Venice Springs Publishing, 212 W. Ironwood Drive, Suite D1-2, Coeur d'Alene, Idaho 83814.

Manufactured in the United States of America

Library of Congress Control Number: 2021901571

ISBN 978-1-7364624-0-9

ISBN 978-1-7364624-1-6 (ebook)

*For my son and daughter,
who have filled my life with incredible joy and laughter.*

Contents

Preface ix
Conclusion 83
Recommended Reading 84
Acknowledgements 85
About the Author 86
Your Added Words of Wisdom:. 87

Preface

Ever since I was old enough to carry on an intelligent conversation, I was fascinated by the advice of those who have lived longer than me. I wondered if they held a secret key to happiness and the real 'meaning of life', because I certainly did not have it. My curiosity would always start out with questions like: What do you do for a living? How long have you been married? Are you happy?

But what I found myself most interested in after obtaining this basic information, was that special piece of advice I was convinced each 'old person' held that could make my life easier so I did not have to learn that same lesson the hard way. I always wanted to find the cheat code to life. How to obtain success and happiness by the fastest means possible.

By the time I reached young adulthood, I thought I already knew everything I needed in life. Little did I know, I was just beginning. My search to find the holy grail of happiness, success, and the meaning of life took a quick turn as I entered college. The world of uncertainty opened as wide as ever, and as graduation day came closer, I realized my future would be dictated by what I had already learned, and the mistakes, failures, and successes yet to be realized. I felt inept, and again craved for the knowledge that would make my life easier. It was then that I came across one of Albert Einstein's most famous quotes: *"The only source of knowledge is experience."* And since I was just entering the 'real world' with little to no experience, I figured my goal of finding a 'life hack' for success and happiness must be found in those who have lived longer than me.

I soon entered a career in federal law enforcement and learned the skills of interviewing others. It made the questioning of those with more experience than me significantly easier, and I never missed an opportunity to keep asking for advice. What I quickly learned was that there was a small clue to finding the holy grail in almost every person who has experienced the hardships and joys that come from living a full life. It is this kernel of advice that I consistently sought from each person I spoke to thereafter, and which I hope to relay to you.

It is important to not just read each piece of advice and move on to the next, but more importantly, to delve deeply into each clue slowly and thoroughly. Just reading the one piece of advice and moving on to the next will only assure that you do not take in the full meaning. It is for this very reason that I have purposefully chosen not to organize the advice contained herein into various categories, as I believe that if you do not know what piece of advice is coming next, you will linger a bit longer on each piece at hand.

Most of the advice within this book was obtained from various unknown sources. However, I have done my very best to acknowledge anyone I could trace to have first written it down. If by chance I have erroneously not given proper credit, I deeply apologize, and will give credit in future editions.

I sincerely hope you will enjoy this book and take away at least one 'life hack' to make things easier and more fulfilling.

Strength in times of crisis comes not from an inborn ability, but rather, is born from experience. Embrace all kinds of crises to harden the steel within.

***

Always answer the telephone with enthusiasm in your voice.

***

When faced with a difficult decision, ponder for a moment over what is the worst that can happen. If you can accept the consequences, then the decision becomes easier.

Find a successful person you admire and want to be like, ask them how they got there, then copy them.

***

Almost everything is negotiable.

***

It only takes the right ingredients at the right time to do something you will regret.

***

TODAY, not tomorrow.

(Need I say more about procrastination?)

'Confidence' is usually only gained by doing things that are uncomfortable or hard, so don't fear the unknown.

**

Always looking forward to the future is a certainty you will miss the present.

**

The most important safety feature in a car is your awareness of your surroundings.

**

Love can only endure in the absence of disrespect.

Happiness is found in not what you think will bring happiness, but what you have at that moment.

***

A bit of fragrance always clings to the hand that gives you roses.

-Ancient Chinese Proverb

***

If you are ever tempted to cheat at anything, realize that no one will remember who won the game, but everyone will remember who cheated.

***

Take charge of your own destiny; rather than relying on luck, circumstance, or other people to forge your future.

You can almost never compliment too much.

***

Identify all your personal "deal breakers" in a relationship, then tell them to your partner. That way if your partner crosses that line, you will know with certainty
it was by choice.

***

Learn CPR, first aid, and how to use an AED; for saving someone's life is the best gift you can give.

Lack of activity destroys the good condition of every human being. While movement and methodical physical exercise save and preserve it.

-Plato

***

Own a pet. The unconditional love will always follow you.

***

Skill in something is acquired through knowledge and effort. Achievement is acquired by adding more effort to skills acquired. Greatness is acquired by adding more effort to simple achievements. Thus, greatness has more to do with effort than any kind of inborn talents, as talents are simply how fast a person is able to improve skill.

- Dr. Angela Duckworth

Always be sure to remember the names of people you will see again.

***

Have a slightly firmer handshake than the one shaking yours.

***

"If it's going to be, it's up to me."

-Unknown Author

***

Realize that your eyes can convey more confidence, honesty, and love than any words ever spoken.

Say "Thank you" often, for appreciation is the key to future assistance.

***

Honk your car horn only when absolutely necessary, and never out of anger.

***

Try to always confirm another person's belief before you disagree with them. By doing so, it assures the person that at least you listened to their point of view first.

Knowledge

When it comes to sports, play with passion or don't play at all.

***

Patience is what checks your emotions and allows reason to work. So be patient when your first emotions take hold, because reason usually takes longer.

***

Respect and appreciation are at the center of every man's needs.

***

Make a point to learn the joys of cooking early in life and the kitchen will always be filled with laughter.

The best predictor of how someone will treat you is how they treated those in their past.

***

See a dentist at least twice a year, and floss regularly – Your smile depends on it!

***

Realize that everyone has needs. The trick is to find a way to meet each other's needs even when they seem to conflict with your own.

***

Understand the basic difference in beliefs of liberals and conservatives so you are able to appeal to both.

Knowledge

Return all things you borrow promptly - plus a little extra.

***

"The time to repair the roof is when the sun is shining." So work on relationship issues when things are good.

-John F. Kennedy

***

Always wear polished dress shoes to work, because a scuff on your shoes, is a scuff on your image.

Ethics is never black and white despite what you may hear, as you will never know all of the facts. Make your decisions based on the outcomes, not your perception of another person's ethics.

***

Before you speak, think of the consequences of your words for they cannot be recalled once spoken.

***

Always keep secrets that others have entrusted with you.

***

If you force something it often breaks, but there is usually an alternate way to get the same thing accomplished.

Never refuse gifts. It will always hurt the giver more than the receiver.

***

When you think you want to push it to the edge, be very careful because the only people who really know where it is are the ones who have gone over.

-Hunter Thompson (Hell's Angels)

***

Write 'thank you' notes promptly.

Every piece of gossip ever told has a second side to it. When you allow yourself to not be biased by the first story, you will most often be closer to the truth.

***

People are ultimately judged by how they treated others.

***

Surprise loved ones with unexpected gifts.

***

Who you know is sometimes more important than what you know.

Knowledge

When working with others, under promise and over-deliver.

***

Accept the responsibility of every decision you make for they were your decisions, not those of others.

***

Admit when you are wrong, rather than making an excuse. It is both cleansing to yourself and others.

***

Shred all documents with your name and address on them to prevent identity theft.

In the middle of difficulty lies an opportunity to learn.

-Albert Einstein

***

If you don't know the answer to a question asked of you, say "I will get back to you" . . . Then do so.

***

Try not to go to bed angry, and make it an unbreakable rule to never argue in bed.

***

Buy quality clothes that won't go out of style. Well-purchased shoes should last a lifetime.

If you have been wronged by someone, try waiting a couple of days to make it right. Often the means of righting the wrong is to let it go. Other times, it involves a means not thought of until days later.

***

Learn the basics of fixing your vehicle so you will never be stranded or deceived by a mechanic.

***

When seeking long-term happiness, understand that humans have evolved to feel more contentment in progressing towards a goal than actually achieving it.

Bake fresh bread often as it will fill your home, your heart, and your stomach.

***

Find a good lawyer before you need one.

(And everyone needs one sooner or later)

***

The greater the trust, the greater the betrayal; and those who know you best will also know how best to betray you.

***

If you are a man, and a woman asks for your help about a serious topic, start out by asking: Do you want me to listen, or do you want me to help fix it?

(Believe me, there is a huge difference!)

Learn the stock market as well as the real estate market, then diversify.

***

Never go back to anyone who treats you with disrespect. . . whether it be a superior, a friend, or a lover.

***

Learn to write well and type fast.

When you want something from someone, make them feel as if they can't lose if they choose what you want. This is much better than trying to convince them it is a 'win-win' situation because in nearly all win-win situations, one person wins more than the other.

***

Always pay credit cards off in full every month. If you can't afford to do so, pay with cash.

***

You feel the way you do because of the thoughts you are thinking.

***

Establish good credit as early in life as possible, and maintain it throughout your life.

Smiles are not only contagious, but are often more persuasive than words.

***

"If you fail to plan, you are planning to fail!"

-Benjamin Franklin

***

Know how to drive a boat and stick shift vehicle even if you don't own one.

(Don't be *'that guy'* who can't when it really counts)

To him whose home is heaven, the whole world is heaven. So always make your house a *'HOME.'*

***

Make an effort to be the first to say *"Hello"* or *"Good evening"*.

***

In school, you are tested on what you learned. In life, you are tested first, then learn from being tested.

***

Respect those who have earned it by addressing them with *"sir"* or *"ma'am"* until you are informed otherwise.

Knowledge

Keep up on current events in the world; however, realize the news media never has *all* the facts.

***

Life is not a dress rehearsal, so make each day count as if it were your last. It just may be.

***

Always keep fire extinguishers in your kitchen and garage.

***

Realize that when you marry a girl, you marry her family.

Fight for what is right, especially when no one else is doing so.

***

Never be afraid to say "I love you" to family.

***

Try to drink tea or hot chocolate instead of coffee – your breath and others will appreciate it.

***

Everyone holds thoughts that are best left unsaid.

Knowledge

Knock before entering a room with a closed door.

(If this isn't obvious, you deserve to be embarrassed.)

***

Learn to do your own taxes, then pay a CPA to do them for you. Their signature on the tax return is worth the peace of mind.

***

Set your clocks at least 5 minutes fast so you're always early; because being 'on time' is still 'late' for many people.

***

Always make sure you have one good night's sleep before making a major decision.

Learn to handle firearms safely.

***

There is almost always room for improvement
– unless you quit.

***

Loaning money to anyone without collateral
is never advisable.

***

Own a national flag and fly it frequently.

Knowledge

Never be without health insurance.

***

Giving people a second chance is considered forgiving, but giving them a third chance is just asking for a fourth.

***

Always ensure your luggage is checked to the correct city.

***

Before signing any document, read the fine print. You will undoubtedly be reading it anyway
after you have been deceived

Never quit a job in haste, and always give at least two weeks' notice.

***

Learn how to fix a toilet, and keep it clean
– for everyone's sake.

***

Holding on to regret only leads to further restless nights.

***

Good posture portrays confidence. Poor posture... well... just looks *really* bad.

Knowledge

If happiness is the goal in life, and some failure is a certainty, then happiness can only be obtained by embracing failure with enthusiasm.

***

Keep lists of things to do, then DO THEM.

***

When in doubt, see a doctor.

***

Never spread rumors, regardless of the temptation.

Criticize in private, praise in public.

***

Avoid telling anyone they look tired or depressed because if they look it, your words are not going to help.

***

Advise someone *tactfully* if they have lint on their clothes or food on their face. If you do, they will return the favor someday.

***

Do not encourage rude or inattentive service by tipping the standard amount.

Knowledge

"Man sacrifices his health to get money, and then sacrifices his money to get back his health."

-*Dalai Lama*

***

One of the best gifts you can give your children is a good role model.

***

Never cut what can be untied.

***

Call your parents/friends frequently. Texting simply does not carry the sound of your voice.

When meeting someone for the first time, resist asking what they do for a living. Enjoy their company without attaching labels.

***

Meet your new neighbors promptly.

***

Service your car frequently, and never let a strange noise go unchecked.

***

The secret to feeling closer to your partner when you're together, is feeling closer when you're apart.

Knowledge

The power of the pen can in fact be mightier than the sword if you truly know how to use it.

-Edward Bulwer-Lytton

***

Make eating right and exercising a way of life.

***

Marriage is about *compromise*. It really is that simple.

***

Always make your home a safe place where you can be silent and still be heard.

Resist criticizing an elder.

***

Use your *good* things before they become your *old* things.

***

If you were to relive your life *exactly* the way you have (every detail in the same succession and sequence), would you choose to do so? If not, change your life now.

-Friedrich Nietzsche

Knowledge

Ensure your wallet/purse always has 'emergency money' and next of kin contact information.

***

Let your loved ones overhear you saying complimentary things about them.

***

Learn to read a map effectively because getting lost is just not fun.

(Unless, of course, you call it "exploring")

***

When you can afford the loss, push your luck.

Never walk away from someone during a quarrel, or hang up on them when angry.

***

Maintain a good filing system. You will thank me later – I promise!

***

If your first emotion of the day is positive, it is statistically more likely that your next one will also be positive.

***

Learn to take quality pictures.

There actually is a lot of truth in the old saying, "Happy wife, happy life."

***

When breaking off a romantic relationship, put forth the effort to remain friends.

***

When there is an injustice in your life, resist the temptation to retaliate in haste. Give yourself time, then formulate a plan with fewer adverse consequences.

***

Success does not always lead to happiness, but happiness will almost always lead to success.

Leave room in your car for a first aid kit, flashlight, flares, and a large blanket.

***

If you let yourself feel jealousy, anger, and regret; you leave no room for happiness.

***

Get all repair estimates in writing *prior* to authorizing work.

***

Share good books with others, as they do little good collecting dust.

Make flexibility one of your best traits.

(And I am not talking about the 'stretching' kind).

***

Small claims court is easier than you think, and *oh so gratifying* when you right the wrong.

***

If you make big decisions while keeping in mind how you want to be remembered, your decisions will more often than not be honorable.

Resist littering – the squirrels are watching.

***

Read to your children early and often as that time together can never be more memorable.

***

Be knowledgeable and respectful of *all* religions.

***

Avoid waiting to be introduced to someone new unless you are royalty.

***

Read parenting books *before* becoming a parent.

Stand when greeting someone or you'll forever be remembered as the person who didn't.

***

Resist the temptation to interrupt as it only conveys disrespect.

***

Prioritize the people around you, how you want to spend your spare time, and things you want for your future. If not, you will find yourself spending your time on things not on that list.

Ensure you always have a way into your car and home in case you get locked out.

***

Learn how to be a good lover, then be the best.

***

Make sure the first words spoken to your partner when you come home are pleasant ones.

***

Going barefoot is good for the soul.

(I know. . . I know)

Remember the three most important things when buying a home or starting a business: LOCATION, LOCATION, LOCATION. It can never be more true.

***

Pack candles on weekend retreats.

***

If there is something bothering you - say so. But do it tactfully.

***

When purchasing real estate and shares of stock, you make your money on 'the buy', not 'the sell.'

If you ever need someone's assistance, start out with the phrase, "I'm hoping you can help me with something."

***

Never use the excuse that 'the alarm clock didn't go off' as it will only solidify a person's belief that you are unreliable. Instead, set two alarm clocks.

***

Respect your parents. You will avoid the guilt that comes years later.

***

Practice a good strong signature early in life as it tells people who you are without meeting you.

Knowledge

Never laugh at anyone's dreams.

***

At least once a year, go someplace you have never been.

***

The worst outcome of a situation does not diminish the decision.
-NFL coach Pete Carroll

***

Learn everything you can about nutrition

Avoid using a mailbox without a lock because the #1 source of identity theft is stolen mail.

***

Backup electronic media regularly, and keep the backups at an alternate secure location. It is too late once you realize you didn't.

***

If someone drops something, pick it up for them. You will always be rewarded with a smile.

***

The joy is in the journey, not the destination.

(Unless you are Leif Erikson)

The Value of Your Name:
"Your name is very valuable; you got it from your father.

Maybe it was all he had to give, but it's yours to use and cherish for as long as you live.

You can lose all else he gave you. It can always be replaced, but a black mark on your name, Son, can never be erased.

So guard it very carefully, for when all is said and done; you'll be glad the name is spotless, when you give it to your son."

-Coach Lou Holtz

***

Respect is gained by taking responsibility for your own actions, even if it involves an apology.

Keep a list of your top achievements, then reflect on them when you doubt your abilities.

***

Mistakes are usually forgivable, but making the same mistake twice is a sign of *intention or incompetence* – both of which are not.

***

There is a difference between having a dream and making your happiness conditional upon your dream coming true.

Knowledge

Life is not complicated - You are born, you live, you die.

It is you that makes life complicated. So if you don't like the way it's going, simplify it.

***

When someone speaks to you, stop what you are doing, then turn and face them.

***

If someone beats you fairly in a game, congratulate them and shake their hand, for a sore loser will find themselves playing alone.

***

Reacting to someone's 'road rage' is never worth it.

Establish a standing line of credit with your bank just in case you need it in an emergency.

(And no... a spring break vacation to Cancun is not an emergency)

***

Every couple of years, take a video of the contents of your home for insurance purposes, then store the copy off-site in the event of a fire.

***

True love can only be found when you allow your partner to become the guardian of your happiness.

Knowledge

With few exceptions, purchasing quality electronics are worth the cost.

***

Learn to dance and play golf as these are two activities you can do at any age.

***

Few relationship failures are a result of only one person.

***

Once you find a trustworthy contractor, always tip them to ensure honest and expeditious service the next time.

Every dollar you spend on healthy food and physical fitness is worth it as your health will cost much more if you don't.

***

Homemade gifts and cards will usually outlast all others – if only in thought.

***

Learn to sing your national anthem, and the history of its origination.

***

Try to only use coupons for items you would normally have purchased anyway.

Knowledge

You don't get what you deserve, but rather,
what you negotiate.

***

"A person isn't who they are during the last conversation you had with them.   They are who they've been throughout your whole relationship."

-*Rainer Maria Rilke* (Bohemian-Austrian Poet)

***

Decide early in life if you believe if 'the end justifies the means' as you will be tested on this belief many times throughout your life.

Luck is when preparation meets opportunity.
Nothing more.

***

Instead of replying *"No"* to a request, challenge
that person to come up with a way so you can say *"Yes."*

***

Try never to criticize, but always encourage.

***

If you can't treat others as you would like to be treated,
then be a hermit.

"Find something you care about, and care deeply."

-Benjamin Asher (Actor)

***

People will remember you by how you make them feel more than what you have accomplished.

***

Compliments lead to friendships, and gibes generally end them.

***

Even the smartest and most responsible people in the world make two or three major mistakes in their lives. So don't be too hard on yourself when you make yours.

"Never underestimate the tendency of human beings to act contrary to their own best interests."

-*Christian Slater* (Actor)

***

The older you get, the faster time seems to pass. Treasure those long days of youth.

***

Marriage is a legal term, but commitment lasts forever.

Knowledge

Every action has a consequence (sometimes good, sometimes bad), so make wise choices.

***

Don't make bets you won't honor.

***

Write 'complaint letters' to seek compensation or invoke change, but never to simply complain.

***

There are only two meanings for the word 'hope':
1) A 'feeling' that tomorrow will be better.
2) A 'resolve' to make tomorrow better.

(Choose the latter)

Learn the difference between being lonely, and being alone.

***

Have a predetermined plan *prior* to being confronted with violence.

***

Learn to hunt, fish, and light a fire in the rain and you will never go hungry.

***

Rejection is just an opportunity to improve.

Knowledge

Pay bills promptly, and try never to handle a piece of mail more than once.

***

Learn to be a master of the grill.

***

Happiness can be found almost anywhere. It is all perspective.

***

Conquer your fears or they will conquer you.

Be extremely tolerant of your elders, especially your parents.

***

If unforeseen circumstances cause you to be late somewhere, always make notification of your tardiness at least five minutes prior to your meeting time.

***

Plan ahead for the important things.

(And everything is important)

***

Jealousy only hurts yourself - no one else.

Remember that respect is both learned and earned.

***

Never burn a bridge you may have to cross.

***

Human nature was cruel when it designed depression to be more comfortable than escaping it. But it is still a choice.

***

A healthy partner relationship requires at least two hugs a day... One in the morning setting the tone for the day and says that you love, appreciate, and respect the other.

The other hug is when you arrive home after having been apart. It will reinforce your sense of partnership and set the tone for the rest of the evening.

Trust nourishes a relationship, fear destroys it.

***

The goal in life is not to reach a preconceived dream, but to be happy while obtaining it.

***

Always have a plan B before executing plan A.

After the death of a loved one, choose one activity that makes you smile about that person, and do it "with them" in spirit after they are gone. You will never be alone when you do that same activity thereafter.

***

Before you are about to start a difficult task, always have a reward waiting for you at the end just in case it doesn't go well.

***

Listen to music *live* whenever possible.

***

"Success is the ability to move from failure to failure without losing enthusiasm."

-Winston Churchill

If something doesn't feel right deep in your gut, think twice before dismissing it.

***

Learn to swim well and tread water for a long time. (Because drowning isn't cool)

***

You don't end up in bad situations, you make bad choices. The reverse is just as true. Good choices lead to good situations.

-*Maeve Wiley* (Sex Education)

If you want a lasting relationship, live within your means.

***

Try to never say "No" to your wife/husband. If you are willing to say *"I do,"* it also means *"I will."* Until you know with certainty you are ready to say I will, don't say I do.

***

Too many people use religion as a crutch when things go bad in their lives. Instead, believe in your power of choice to determine your destiny and you will find religion that much more fulfilling.

You'll never know when it's the last time you'll kiss a loved one until it is.

***

Non-buyer's remorse is more often worse than buyer's remorse. So if you can afford to do so, buy it, then return or sell it if you chose wrongly.

***

Emotional and financial security are key ingredients to preserving a relationship.

***

If you ever find yourself in a frightening situation and you must prevail; remember that fear is a reaction, and courage is a decision.

-*Winston Churchill*

Make getting enough sleep a priority because sleep-deprived people perform worse than drunk people.

***

Teach your children to play chess as it mimics the very difficult choices they will face in life, and how to overcome them to be successful.

***

The world rarely appreciates the good deeds you do, but will criticize the one bad thing you do.
So be the person who does recognize the good deeds of others each day and you will bring joy to those around you.

Choose hard things for an easy life later, and easy things for a hard life later.

- *T. Harv Eker* (Motivational Speaker)

***

Don't believe everything you hear, as there is always "the rest of the story."

-*Paul Harvey*

***

In business, your *network* really is your net worth.

If you have an office, fill it with things that make you smile, rather than plaques of achievements.

***

'Grit' is the single best predictor of success for those who have mastered skills; for without grit, greatness is fleeting.

A person possessing 'Grit' is best defined as one who has these four traits: Passion, Determination, Direction, and Perseverance.

Road map to *Success* summarized:

1) Knowledge + Effort = Skill

2) Skill + Effort = Achievement

3) Achievement + Effort = Greatness

4) Greatness + Grit = Success

- Dr. Angela Duckworth

Listen to "taps" every Veterans Day and you will understand what they gave.

***

Develop a 'life philosophy' of exactly what you want out of your life. Without a philosophy, there can be no direction for your life.

***

Try to discard any goals that do not make your top five priorities for they will only serve as distractions that eat away time and energy from the top five goals.

-Warren Buffett

Knowledge

Always give your best to your partner because if your best is not good enough, you won't look back with regret should they choose to leave.

***

There are several things you can't get back in life...

-Harsh words after they are spoken.

-An opportunity after it is missed.

-Trust after it is lost.

-Time after it is gone.

***

If you stay at someone's house as a guest, always strip the bed and leave a 'thank you' note with a small personal gift on the bed thanking them.

Realize that it is your *perception* of future consequences that drives one to be either optimistic or pessimistic.

***

Read the book *The Five Love Languages: How to Express Heartfelt Commitment to Your Mate* by Dr. Gary Chapman.

(It doesn't get much clearer than this!)

***

If you keep searching for ways to change your situation, you will likely have a better chance to do so than if you stop searching.

"Whether you think you can, or think you can't - you're right."

-Henry Ford

***

Never leave a candle burning in an empty room.

***

People gravitate towards those who smile as it indicates confidence and diffuses anxiety.

***

Avoid the statement, *"I don't have enough time,"* as it usually means *"I don't want to"* for the person hearing it.

Everyone keeps some secrets. Respect those your partner chose to keep, and they will respect yours. Then trust your partner to let you know if their secrets
will adversely affect you.

***

If you expect a partner to change, you can also expect to be changing partners.

***

Learn basic self-defense tactics early as you will undoubtedly need them at some point.

Knowledge

Tread lightly, but carry a heavy stick. And if you must use that stick in defense of yourself or others, strike first and strike hard.

***

Always have flowers in your home.

***

Babies don't need pacifiers, they need nurturing caring parents who understand their needs.

***

Excuses are reserved for those who don't want it bad enough.

Most people are born with at least one natural talent, but identifying it is not so simple. So until you discover yours, try to become good at something along the way. Don't take it for granted and don't betray it because
it may just be your gift after all.

***

Make a bucket list and update it often. Then make it shorter.

***

The best children are raised by the best parents.

***

Always wear pressed clothes to work.

(Your co-workers notice)

If you don't truly understand why a relationship failed, you will soon find yourself in yet another failed relationship.

***

Always say "excuse me" if you bump into someone, even if it was their fault.

***

You can't truly listen if you are talking.

***

If your child agrees to sign up for an extracurricular activity, insist they see it through until the end of the season.

Don't buy cheap tools unless you are willing to replace them.

***

If you go to bed with a plan, you often wake up with a better solution.

***

Avoid bad breath, and check it often.

(Just sayin' . . .)

***

Motivation is halfway to finishing.

Micromanagement is the surest sign of poor management.

***

"Never look down on anyone else, unless you are helping them up."

-Jesse Jackson

***

Change air conditioner filters every 3 months.

(Unless you really like breathing moldy air)

Be cautious of giving unsolicited advice to others.

***

Mastering something is little more than stringing together rather mundane tasks in repetition.

***

Life is full of fun, challenging, trying, and sometimes seemingly impossible choices. The "consequences" are sometimes amazing when you choose wisely.

***

Set high expectations for children and teenagers, then give them the support and encouragement to meet those expectations.

"It is hard to fail, but is worse never to have tried to succeed."

-Theodore Roosevelt

***

Seek marriage 'advice' before getting married, or it will be called 'counseling' later.

***

"Ah, make the most of what we yet may spend, Before we too into the Dust descend."

-Omar Khayyam (Persian Philosopher)

Stay humble because in the end, your hole in the ground is the same size as everyone else's.

Conclusion

Undoubtedly, entire books have been written and published about nearly every piece of advice I have summarized for you above. I would encourage you to seek out those references if you find one particular piece of advice meaningful or helpful. Below you will find a list of my personal favorite recommended readings for more in-depth life advice.

Furthermore, I firmly believe there is no greater gift one can give a young adult than the advice you too have obtained during your own lifetime. This is the true gift I want to give my children, and I hope whoever reads this book takes the time to add their own advice to this list as you gain knowledge and experience. Blank pages have been provided at the end of this book for your own words of wisdom, so that your clues to that holy grail will not be lost in the dust of time.

I wish the best for anyone who took the time to read this compilation of treasures, and uses this 'knowledge' to guide them to a prosperous, fulfilling, and happy life.

Recommended Reading

Chapman, Gary. *The Five Love Languages: How to Express Heartfelt Commitment to Your Mate.* Chicago: Northfield Publishing, 1992.

Duckworth, Angela. *Grit – The Power of Passion and Perseverance.* New York: Scribner Publishing, 2016.

Gray, John. *Men Are from Mars, Women Are from Venus.* New York: HarperCollins Publishing, 1992.

Cove, Stephen. *The 7 Habits of Highly Effective People.* New York: Free Press Publishing, 1989.

Allen, David. *Getting Things Done – The Art of Stress-Free Productivity.* New York: Penguin Books Publishing, 2001.

Hendrix, Harville. *Getting the Love You Want – A Guide for Couples.* New York: St. Martin's Publishing, 1988.

Kennedy, Gavin. *Everything is negotiable – How to get the best deal every time.* New York: Random House Publishing, 1982.

Acknowledgements

I cannot imagine going through life all over again without being armed with the incredible advice provided to me by my amazing parents. Their experience and life advice (which as a teen I was not ready to hear from them), provided me the perfect foundation to live a truly happy life.

I am also especially grateful to my brother Peter, and my good friends Steven Kapellas and Father Richard Poole (Airforce Chaplain), for all the countless hours spent with me debating the meaning of life and how to achieve success and happiness. It was their talks, sometimes going way too late into the evening, that ultimately drove me to start writing down this list of knowledge to pass on to my children.

It is important I mention a few other very influential people who have come into my life and changed it forever. So a special thanks goes to my ROTC commander Colonel Denny McMonigle, Assistant U.S. Attorney Earl Hicks (Eastern District of Washington), Professor George Gollin (University of Illinois), Al Turtle (Relationship counselor), and Alvin Stern (World War II combat veteran) who have all inspired me in more ways than can be imagined.

A special thanks goes out to all of the rest of you who have provided me, and the readers, with your secrets to success and happiness even after your words have outlasted your existence on this earth.

And lastly (but most importantly), I wish to recognize my loving and caring wife who always backed me when I tried to sneak in just one more piece of advice for our children at the dinner table or on a road trip. She taught me more about patience, understanding, and relationships than any other.

About the Author

John E. Neirinckx II is a retired federal law enforcement agent who spent most of his career in the U.S. Secret Service surrounded by world leaders, successful sports figures, famous actors/actresses, and multi-millionaires where he observed and gained their insight into success and happiness. He also spent the latter part of his career in the Department of Veterans Affairs where he interviewed countless combat war veterans in search of their words of wisdom. John is currently the owner of a land development company and spends much of his free time wandering among the tall pines of Idaho. He shares his life with his wife, two teenage children, and a Goldendoodle named Suki.

Your Added Words of Wisdom:

www.ingramcontent.com/pod-product-compliance
Lightning Source LLC
Chambersburg PA
CBHW030913080526
44589CB00010B/286